The Journey Of Whispers Into Words

Meera Bhalani

BookLeaf Publishing

India | USA | UK

Presentation by *BookLeaf Publishing*

Web: www.bookleafpub.com

E-mail: info@bookleafpub.com

ISBN: 9789363301658

First edition 2024

|| सत्यम् शिवम् सुंदरम् ||

"Satyam Shivam Sundaram"

*Dedicated to the pursuit of truth, the embrace
of divinity, and the celebration of beauty.*

ACKNOWLEDGEMENT

Creating "A Journey of Whispers into Words" has been an incredible experience, one that wouldn't have been possible without the support and encouragement of many wonderful individuals.

A special thanks to my editor for your keen eye and thoughtful suggestions, and my publisher for believing in this project and bringing it to life.

Firstly, I would like to express my deepest gratitude to my family for their unwavering support. Your love and support have been my foundation. To my parents, for instilling in me a love for literature and the power of words. To my siblings, for always believing in my dreams.

To my dear daughters Hemansi and Khushi, thank you for giving me the gift of incredible motherhood. Your love and inspiration have been a guiding light in my life and in the creation of this book.

"Your laughter is the melody of my days, and your wonder paints the canvas of my soul.
Being the bright star in my night sky, guiding my pen with the pure light of your love and dreams."

A special thanks to my niece, Shivani, for inspiring me with your boundless energy and enthusiasm. Your joy and zest for life have been a source of inspiration, and your belief in me has been a driving force throughout this journey. The title of this book, "A Journey of Whispers into Words," is a testament to how the quiet moments we shared, filled with your laughter and stories, transformed into the written words of these poems.

I am deeply grateful to my friends who offered their time and insight, providing valuable feedback and encouragement. Your honest critiques and kind words have helped shape this book into what it is today.

Finally, to every reader who picks up this book, thank you for joining me on this poetic journey. Your appreciation for the written word gives life to these whispers turned into words.

With heartfelt thanks,
Meera

PREFACE

In the silent spaces between the hustle and bustle of everyday life, there exists a sanctuary where whispers are born. These whispers, soft and subtle, are the seeds of thoughts, emotions, and stories waiting to be nurtured into words. "A Journey of Whispers into Words" is a collection that chronicles this delicate transformation, capturing the essence of those fleeting moments and giving them a voice.

This anthology is more than just a compilation of poems; it is an exploration of the human spirit. Each poem represents a unique whisper—an intimate conversation between the heart and the soul. These whispers are often the unsaid, the overlooked, and the quietly profound. They speak of love in its many forms, of the gentle caress of a morning breeze, of the stunning beauty, and of the enduring strength found in resilience. There are verses that celebrate the exuberance of new beginnings, capturing the thrill of first love and the promise of dreams.

The journey this collection invites you on is both personal and universal. It is a path that meanders through the inner landscapes of the soul, reflecting the shared experiences that bind us all. As you read these poems, you may find echoes of your own whispers, the quiet thoughts that linger at the edge of consciousness, waiting to be acknowledged and embraced.

Through the art of poetry, "A Journey of Whispers into Words" seeks to illuminate the beauty found in both the spoken and the unspoken. It is a celebration of the power of words to heal, to inspire and to connect. Each poem is a testament to the enduring strength of the human spirit and the endless journey of discovery that life offers.

Thank you for embarking on this journey with me. May these words resonate with you, offering solace, inspiration and a reminder that even the softest whisper can leave an indelible mark on the heart.

Welcome to "A Journey of Whispers into Words."

A Journey Of The Poem Book

In a quiet nook, where muses dream,
A poet's heart begins to gleam.
With quill in hand and thoughts unchained,
A journey starts, where words are gained.

Each page a path, each verse a stride,
Through landscapes vast, where musings hide.
From dawn's first light to twilight's hush,
In ink and rhyme, the heartbeats rush.

Beginnings spark with eager fire,
A dream, a hope, a soul's desire.
The first steps tread on untouched ground,
Where silent whispers now resound.

Along the way, companions meet,
In lines and stanzas, rhythms sweet.
They share the load, the joy, the pain,
In every word, their spirits wane.

Challenges arise, the road is steep,
The climb is hard, the valleys deep.
Yet in the struggle, strength is found,
As voices soar from the battleground.

With every verse, transformation comes,
The poet's heart, it beats and drums.
Through metamorphosis, they find,
A clearer voice, a sharper mind.

Reflections cast in twilight's glow,
A mirror where true selves show.
Wisdom gathered, lessons learned,
On every page, a story turned.

The journey's end, a homeward trail,
With stories told, where dreams prevail.
In boundless realms of ink and thought,
A poet's journey, richly wrought.

In quiet nooks, where muses dream,
The poet's heart continues to gleam.
With quill in hand and thoughts unchained,
New journeys start, where words are gained.

Mother's Lullaby

Sleep, my darling, close your eyes,
In my arms, the whole world lies.
Hear my whispers, soft and sweet,
Lullabies for you, my treat.

Hush now, child! The night is near,
In my love, there's nothing to fear.
Dream of skies so blue and wide,
Feel my heart right by your side.

Murmurs turn to words of grace,
As you grow, time can't erase
The wisdom wrapped in love's embrace,
Guiding you through life's vast space.

Tiny hands will grow so strong,
Years will pass, but love stays long.
In your heart, my voice will stay,
Guiding you along your way.

Feel the mumble, gentle, true,
Carrying love from me to you.
Through the years, both near and far,
You'll remember who you are.

As you blossom, day by day,
In your heart, my words will stay.
Songs of love, of hope, of light,
Guiding you through the darkest night.

In your dreams, you'll hear me still,
Urging you to uphold your will
In your heart, my love will shine,
A guiding star, forever thine.

Now you stand, wearing strong smiles,
Facing all the world's trials.
Know my love is always near,
In your heart, forever clear.

Sleep, my darling, rest your head,
With my words, be gently led.
From my whispers, strength will grow,
Love and wisdom always flow.

Father's Love

In the stillness of dawn, a whisper is born,
A gentle murmur, soft and warm.
It drifts through the air, unseen, unheard,
A tender promise, a heartfelt word.

Father and daughter, a bond so tight,
In the quiet moments of morning light.
He mumbles to her tales of old,
Of knights and dragons, brave and bold.

Her laughter rings, a melody sweet,
Tiny feet dancing to an invisible beat.
In his arms, she finds her place,
A world of safety, love, and grace.

Wonders turn to words as days go by,
From bedtime stories to questions of "why?"
He guides her gently, with wisdom and care,
A lighthouse standing, always there.

Through joy and dreams expressed
In his embrace, she finds her best.
Her tiny hand in his, a perfect clasp,
Together, they journey, life's gentle grasp.

Years will pass, as they always do,
But the secret message remains true.
For in each story, in each shared glance,
Lies a love that forever will enhance.

Father and daughter, a timeless tale,
A bond of care that will never pale.
In every word, in every tender sign,
Lives a bond, eternal and divine.

From the first step, she takes to her first broken
heart,
He's there to hold her, never apart.
Teaching her the strength to stand on her own,
While always ensuring she's never alone.

Through school days, achievements, and the
tears that flow,
In every triumph and every low.
A silent strength, a guiding hand,
In life's ever-shifting, drifting sand.

On starlit nights, with skies so clear,
They share their dreams, their hopes, their fears.
He listens intently, with patience, with grace,
Each word a treasure, each smile a trace.

As she grows older, spreads her wings wide,
In him, she knows, she can always confide.
For the murmur of childhood, now grown into words,
Are echoes of love always heard.

In the tapestry of life, a father's role,
Is to nurture, to cherish, to make her whole.
From whispers to words, from cradle to grown,
A journey of love, a bond clearly shown.

So as they walk this path, side by side,
With love as their guide, and hearts open wide.
A father and daughter,
Forever entwined, love defined.

Colors Of Childhood

Fields of golden sunlight, where dreams take
flight,
There lives a world of wonder, pure and bright.
With laughter like the morning dew, so clear,
The heart of childhood, unburdened by fear.

In eyes that twinkle with the stars' own light,
Imagination soars to boundless heights.
Each day a canvas, painted fresh and new,
With colors of a world that's pure and true.

Tiny hands explore the world so wide,
With curiosity as their gentle guide.
Every step a journey, bold and free,
Inspiring hearts with their simplicity.

Through whispers of the breeze and songs of
birds,
A melody of innocence is heard.
A symphony of dreams yet to be spun,
In the soft glow of each rising sun.

Let us cherish this sweet, fleeting time,
When every moment is a perfect rhyme.
For in the laughter of the young and free,
Lies the essence of what we're meant to be.

So, may we guard this gift with tender care,
Inspiring all with love beyond compare.
For in the heart of every child's delight,
Shines the promise of a world made right.

Their tiny footsteps on a path unknown,
A journey where their spirits have flown.
With wonder at each glance, they teach us how,
To live in the beauty of the here and now.

In simple joys, they find their way,
Turning ordinary into magic each day.
Their innocence a beacon, shining bright,
Guiding us through the darkest night.

Let us learn from their untainted view,
To see the world as fresh and new.
For in the heart of childhood's embrace,
We find our true and sacred place.

Heartstrings

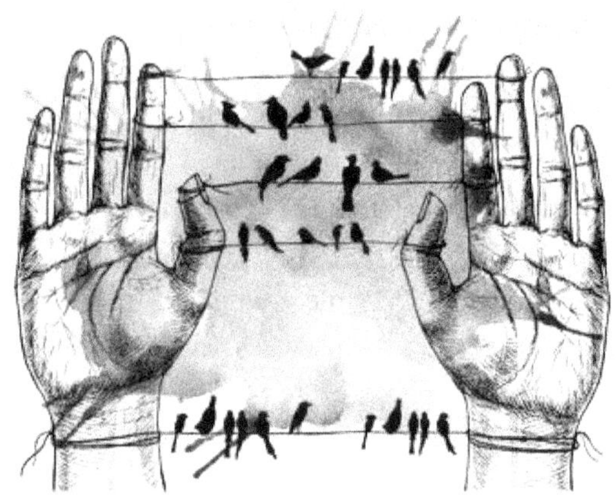

Through the hustle of days and quiet of nights,
We navigate life with all its delights.
In moments small, yet deeply true,
We find the bonds that help us through.

A helping hand when times are tough,
A patient ear when words aren't enough.
In shared stories and simple acts,
We forge connections that truly impact.

Through forgiveness sought and lessons learned,
In each other's flaws, acceptance earned.
With patience and understanding, we grow,
In imperfect harmony, our love does show.

So, here's to the journey, both smooth and rough,
In building relationships that are strong enough.
With laughter, tears, and everything in between,
Together, inspiring moments, unseen.

Through trials faced and victories won,
In each other's glories, we find our sun.
With dreams pursued and goals achieved,
Together, our bond is deeply relived.

In moments of joy and challenges faced,
Our unity strengthens, never displaced.
With gratitude for the love we share,
In every hug and smile, we declare:

That in this journey, hand in hand,
We inspire each other to understand.
Through kindness shown and respect earned,
In this togetherness that our spirits yearned.

Threads Of Gold

In the tapestry of life, we weave,
A bond so strong, it's hard to believe.
From laughter shared to tears we've shed,
With every step, our spirits are led.

Through thick and thin, in joy and strife,
You've been my rock, my guiding light.
With every word and every deed,
You've shown me strength and met my need.

We dream together, hearts aligned,
In you, my friend, pure gold I find.
With every challenge, every test,
We do inspire and give our best.

Our friendship's like a boundless sky,
With countless stars that light up high.
Together, we are brave and true,
Soaring high and shining bright.

When darkness falls and hope seems thin,
Your voice, a beacon, draws me in.
With courage, love, and endless grace,
You lift me from the darkest place.

In moments when the world stands still,
Your presence gives me strength and will.
Together, we are fierce and true,
A friendship rare, just me and you.

So here's to you, my cherished friend,
May this bond never see an end.
Inspire, support, and always be,
The best of friends, eternally.

Fading Footprints

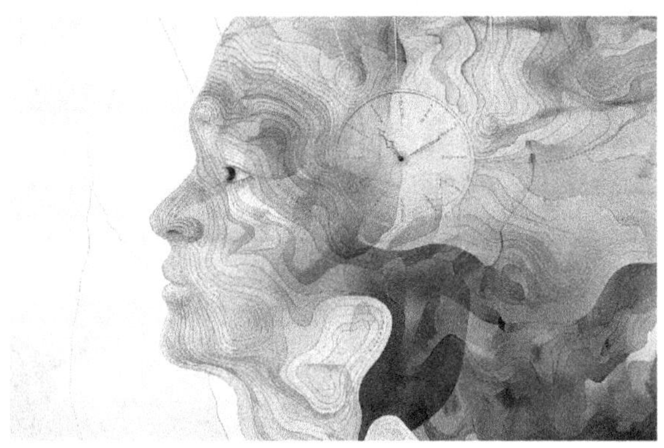

In the corridors of time, where shadows grow,
Memories linger like echoes of old,
Fragments of youth in sepia tones,
In the attic of my mind, they find their home.

Aged hands tremble, tracing lines,
Etched by years, by laughter, by tears,
Faces once clear now softened by mist,
Lost in the passage where moments persist.

Time's gentle thief steals moments away,
Leaving behind echoes that gently sway,
In the silence of night, they come to play,
A symphony of life in a dance so frail.

Yet amidst the fading, a spark remains,
A flame that flickers, that never wanes,
For memories, though fragile, hold fast their sway,
An ode to the past, in hues of gray.

So, let us welcome this twilight's embrace,
Where memories dance in a quiet grace,
For in aging's touch, we find solace deep,
In the stories we keep, as old memories sleep.

In the vaults of my heart, where time is kind,
Memories bloom like flowers in the mind,
Each petal a story, each bloom a delight,
In the garden of memories, forever bright.

Through the ebb and flow of life's endless stream,
Memories gleam like stars in a cosmic dream,
Each constellation a tale, each twinkling light
Guiding my spirit through the darkest night.

Dreams To Reality

Within quiet depths, dreams reside,
A world unfolds, where hopes abide.
Echoes of what could be, so bright,
Glimmers of stars in the darkest night.

Through the mist of doubt and fear,
We chase our dreams, ever near.
Each step a bridge from sky to ground,
Where dreams take form, profound.

In the tapestry of time and fate,
We weave our dreams, never late.
With courage as our guiding light,
We paint our dreams in colors bright.

From whispers soft to voices strong,
Dreams to reality, where we belong.
With each heartbeat, with each breath,
We journey on, defying death.

For dreams are seeds we plant with care,
Watered by hope, nurtured by dare.
And as we reach towards the sky,
Dreams to reality, they never die.

So let us dream, and let us dare,
To chase our dreams beyond compare.
For in the journey, in the flight,
Dreams to reality, shining bright.

Let our hearts be fearless, our spirits high,
As dreams unfold beneath the sky.
For in each dream, a world is spun,
Dreams to reality, we are one.

With perseverance as our steadfast guide,
We conquer doubts that may reside.
With each challenge faced, we grow strong,
Turning dreams into our lifelong song.

Love Letter

In the hush of twilight's embrace,
Where echoes flow in graceful rhythm.
I pen these lines with love anew,
Wrapped in thoughts of only you.

Each word a brushstroke, soft and kind,
Painting dreams upon my mind.
In the quiet hum of evening's sigh,
Your essence whispers, as if close by.

Through valleys deep and fields of gold,
My love for you, forever bold.
In every curve of each letter's trace,
A promise of eternal embrace.

For in your eyes, a universe unfolds,
Where stories of our love are told.
In every sentence, a melody's sigh,
Our throbbing hearts, soaring high.

With each phrase, a cherished tale,
Of how your love has set sail.
In every thought, a tender art,
Sculpted from the depths of heart.

So let this letter gently flow,
With love that only you can know.
For in these lines, a soul laid bare,
A testament to the love we share.

Music

All notes that dance upon the air,
Music weaves its spell so rare.
A melody, a rhythm's beat,
Stirring souls with each repeat.

Strings that choir, drums that roar,
Music speaks what words adore.
Harmony in every strain,
Echoes of joy, of loss, of pain.

From symphonies to lullabies,
Music paints the endless skies.
A language known in every land,
Guiding hearts with a gentle hand.

In the silence, music blooms,
Filling rooms with sweet perfumes.
From flute to violin's embrace,
Each instrument finds its place.

A symphony of colors bright,
Painting day and soothing night.
Lyrics spun like a golden thread,
Weaving tales from heart to head.

From jazz that swings with playful flair,
To ballads soft as mumbled prayer.
Music binds us, heart to heart,
A symphony of every part.

So let us listen, let us sway,
To melodies that gently play.
For in music's timeless art,
We find solace in the heart.

So let the music play and flow,
In its embrace, we all may grow.
For in its chords, we find release,
A timeless melody of peace.

Notes Beneath The Noise

In the hush of dawn's first light,
Silence speaks with soft delight.
No words are needed, none to say,
In quiet, thoughts can gently sway.

A stillness holds the world in place,
In silence, we can find our space.
Echoes of the soul, profound,
In silence, all our dreams are found.

In the heart of silence, a symphony begins,
Notes of peace and calm, where silence wins.
A gentle breeze whispers through the trees,
Carrying dreams on the wings of ease.

Awakening

But silence too holds a secret spark,
A quiet strength in the depths of the dark.
From its depths, a song starts to rise,
A rhythm that ignites, that defies.

Resonance

Silence dances with unseen grace,
In its embrace, energies interlace.
The quietude, a canvas so vast,
Paints dreams in hues that forever last.

Vibrant Harmony

Then, from the stillness, passion springs,
A crescendo of life, where spirit sings.
In the quietude, hear the beat,
A symphony of silence, pure and sweet.

Eternal Serenade

Amidst the silence, echoes of the past,
Whispers of memories that forever last.
Yet in silence, the future is born anew,
A melody of hope, vibrant and true.

Celestial Cadence

Stars above, in silent ballet,
Dance to rhythms unseen, night and day.
In their silence, cosmic symphonies play,
A universe alive, in silence they sway.

Embrace of Quiet

Embrace the silence; let it unfold,
In its depths, mysteries untold.
From silence springs courage and might,
A symphony of life, in silent flight.

Rain And Ocean

Softly falls the gentle rain,
Whispering secrets on the plain.
Drops that dance on leaves and land,
Gather strength, a journey planned.

Trickling down a silver thread,
Joining creeks on paths ahead.
Through valleys deep and meadows green,
Gathering speed, a mighty stream.

Rushing rivers, swift and free,
Carving paths to the waiting sea.
Roaring with a joyful cry,
To the ocean, they'll soon fly.

Waves embrace the newfound friend,
Raindrops mingle without end.
In the vast and endless blue,
A journey complete, forever true.

Upon the shore, where waters meet,
Tides recede with a gentle beat.
Sunlight kisses, waves in play,
Reflecting skies of azure day.

Beneath the surface, mysteries unfold,
In coral gardens, vibrant and bold.
Fish in schools like silver gleam,
In this liquid world, a tranquil dream.

From distant lands and skies above,
Comes a gift of life and love.
Rain to the ocean, hand in hand,
Nature's dance, forever grand.

As stars above and moonlight gleams,
The ocean whispers ancient dreams.
Of raindrops fallen, pure and free,
Merging with the endless sea.

The Light's Trail

In the journey of light, shadows fade away,
Guiding us through the darkest night to day.
Each beam whispers tales of hope and might,
A symphony of courage, blazing bright.

From dawn's embrace to twilight's glow,
Light dances through paths we dare to sow.
In its warmth, resilience finds its birth,
Unveiling truths buried deep in earth.

Celebrate the journey, let the radiance lead,
Through valleys of doubt and fields of need.
For in every gleam, a lesson learned,
In every spark, a bridge is turned.

So let your spirit rise on wings of flame,
Rejoice the light, and never be the same.
For in its glow, the world unfolds anew,
A testament to the strength within you.

In the tapestry of time, light's endless song,
Ignites the soul, where dreams belong.
Through trials faced with steadfast grace,
It paints tomorrow's hopeful treasure.

Miracle

In the quiet dawn of morning light,
A whisper of the day's first sight,
A miracle unfolds so bright,
In the gentle break of night.

A tiny seed beneath the earth,
Unseen, it waits for its time of birth,
A miracle of priceless worth,
Emerging in its silent mirth.

A child's laughter, pure and clear,
A sound that chases doubt and fear,
A miracle so precious, near,
Reminds us why we're here.

The ocean's waves, in constant flow,
A rhythm that we've come to know,
A miracle, it starts to show,
In every ebb and gentle blow.

The stars that dot the night's expanse,
In them, we find our dreams and chances,
A miracle in every glance,
A cosmic, timeless, silent dance.

In every heartbeat, breath, and sigh,
In every teardrop, we might cry,
A miracle beneath the sky,
In every life that passes by.

So let us cherish, hold, and see,
These miracles that come to be,
In every moment, wild and free,
A wondrous, vast infinity.

In every challenge that we face,
A chance to grow, to find our place,
A miracle of strength and grace,
To rise above and set the pace.

Inner voice

In the stillness of the soul's deep well,
Where echoes of thoughts softly dwell,
There lies a murmur, clear and true,
A voice that speaks of what we knew.

It hums gently through the night,
Guiding us with its quiet light,
In moments hushed, when the day is gone,
It sings to us, a timeless song.

Through doubts that cloud and fears that creep,
It holds the secrets we can keep,
A compass true, in times of strife,
It leads us to our inner life.

In mumble soft, yet bold and strong,
It tells us where we do belong,
With every beat, our hearts align,
To hear this voice, so pure, divine.

So listen close, within your heart,
For there, the melody will impart,
They weave a tale of who we are,
Guiding us, both near and far.

Embrace the voice that's always near,
For in its words, there's naught to fear,
It speaks of dreams that yet unfold,
A story timeless, still untold.

In the depths of quiet, find your way,
The inner voice has much to say,
In silence, wisdom's path unfurls,
The voice within shapes all our worlds.

Meditation Among The Stars

Under the night's quiet blanket,
When the stars begin to gleam,
I close my eyes and take a flight,
Into the cosmic dream.

The universe, a vast expanse,
A tapestry of light,
In meditation's silent dance,
I journey through the night.

Galaxies swirl in mystic dance,
Nebulas softly glow,
In this celestial expanse,
My spirit starts to flow.

Each star, a point of ancient lore,
A distant light guides the way
In cosmic meditation's core,
I find out who I am.

Beyond the Earth, beyond the skies,
In quiet contemplation,
The cosmos seen through inner eyes,
Sync with my meditation vibes.

Timeless, boundless, infinite,
A realm of endless wonder,
In the cosmic quiet night,
I feel my spirit's thunder.

Connected to the universe,
In every breath I take,
Join my cosmic flow,
I am awake, awake.

Eternal Essence

Where sacred realms are, there spirits soar,
A bond divine forevermore.
Beyond the veil of time and place,
An endless love, a boundless grace.

Through whispers soft of ancient trees,
In murmured songs of timeless seas,
We find each other, soul to soul,
In every part, we are the whole.

The stars above, they weave our tale,
In constellations, bright and pale.
Each twinkling light, a vow renewed,
A testament to love imbued.

In every dawn, in every dusk,
Our spirits meld in purest trust.
No shadow falls, no night can hide,
The light within, where we abide.

Eternal dance of light and shade,
In sacred bond, we're gently swayed.
The cosmos sings our love's refrain,
A melody that knows no pain.

In realms divine, our hearts align,
A love eternal, pure, sublime.
Forever joined, in endless flight,
Our spirits shine in boundless light.

In every heartbeat, every breath,
We transcend life, we conquer death.
Our souls, entwined, forever soar,
A divine connection, evermore.

God's Creation

In the beginning, when time was but a dream,
God whispered life into the cosmic stream.
Stars were kindled in the velvet night,
Casting their glow, a celestial sight.

Mountains rose from the ocean's caress,
Valleys carved by time's gentle grace.
Forests whispered with ancient trees,
Leaves dancing softly in the breeze.

Rivers meandered through verdant plains,
Reflecting the sky's ever-changing stains.
Oceans roared with a mighty call,
Holding secrets in their depths, both great and
small.

Birds took flight with colors so bright,
Painting the dawn with their joyous flight.
Creatures roamed, both great and small,
Each one a masterpiece, crafted by the All.

Man and woman, in God's own mold,
With hearts of courage and spirits bold,
Given dominion, yet tasked to care,
For all creation, both here and there.

In every bloom, in every song,
God's creation sings, "To Him we belong."
A fabric woven with love and grace,
Reflecting the Creator in every space.

So, let us cherish this wondrous land,
Every grain of sand, every strand,
For in God's creation, we find our place,
A testament to His boundless grace.

Beneath the sky, so vast and wide,
We walk this earth with hearts open wide.
With love and kindness, let us sow,
In God's creation, let our spirits grow.

Journey Of A Soul

In realms unseen, where echoes fade,
The soul embarks, its path unmade.
Through veils of time, it wanders far,
Seeking truths beneath each star.

In dreams it roams, in silence hears,
Whispers of forgotten years.
From dusk to dawn, through endless night,
It quests for meaning, seeks the light.

Through trials faced and fears unfurled,
It finds within the heart, the world.
In every tear, in every sigh,
The soul awakens and learns to fly.

Beyond the veil, where shadows play,
It dances on through endless days.
Eternal journey, without end,
The soul, a universe, transcends.

In the quiet chambers of the heart,
Where shadows blend and worlds unite.
The soul, a seeker, yearns to trace
The paths of wisdom, time, and grace.

Through valleys deep and mountains high,
It wanders 'neath the boundless sky,
In search of truths that softly gleam
Like whispers of an ancient dream.

In moments still, it finds its song,
Amidst the silence, where thoughts belong,
Reflecting stars that softly burn,
In every soul, a light to yearn.

Through trials etched in sorrow's gaze,
It learns to navigate the maze,
Of joy and pain, of loss and gain,
Each step, a note in life's refrain.

And as it journeys, hand in hand,
With fate and destiny's demands,
It finds within, beyond the strife,
The essence of its endless life.

For in the journey, far and wide,
It learns to love, to seek, to guide,
And in the tapestry of time,
The soul unfolds, sublime, divine.

Universe Unveiled

Behold the universe, a Gobelin divine,
Where stars ignite like jewels that shine,
In realms of darkness, galaxies unfold,
Stories of creation, timeless and bold.

From nebula's birth to supernova's flare,
Cosmic symphonies fill the air,
Planets spin in graceful ballet,
In the cosmic theater, night and day.

Black holes sing their silent song,
Bridging worlds where time is strong,
Yet in this vast and boundless sky,
Hope and wonder never die.

For every atom, every spark,
Echoes the universe's grand remark,
That from stardust we are made,
In its splendor, our paths laid.

So gaze upon the heavens bright,
Embrace the stars' eternal light,
For in this cosmic dance we see,
The beauty of what's meant to be.

In the cradle of the cosmos, where dreams take
flight,
Galaxies bloom like flowers in the night,
Each star a story, mumble soft and low,
Of ancient mysteries, we yearn to know.

Oh, what tales the universe does weave,
Of gravity's twirl and particles that cleave,
Through space and time, we wander free,
Explorers of this cosmic sea.

For every twinkling star above,
Whispers secrets of hope and love,
In the vast expanse, we find our place,
Awed by the beauty of infinite space.

Moments

In fleeting hours, we find our joy,
Moments we cherish, no time to destroy.
A dance of sunlight, a sighing breeze,
Celebrate these moments as they tease.

Laughter cascades like gentle rain,
Memories painted on the heart's plain.
In every heartbeat, a story told,
Celebrate the now, before it's old.

For time, a fleeting, precious friend,
Moments cherished, to no end.
In each pile, in every smile,
Celebrate the exile in life's mile.

So raise a toast to love and light,
To every delight, flaming bright.
In this dance of life, where we roam,
Celebrate the moment, make it home.

In the delicate tones of morning light,
The world awakens, fresh and bright.
Dreams unfurl like petals in bloom,
In every challenge, a chance to groom.

With courage as our guiding star,
We journey on, no matter how far.
In every stumble, lessons learned,
Strength renewed, bridges formed.

For in the fabric of our days,
Hope and courage light our ways.
In every story yet to be told,
Love and kindness, hearts unfold.

Gratitude's Grace

In the silent first light, when the world's at rest,
I count my blessings; I feel truly blessed.
For every sunrise that paints the sky,
For every gentle breeze that whispers by.

Gratitude, a gift from heart to soul,
A melody that makes the spirit whole.
In each flower's bloom, in each bird's call,
In every moment, big or small.

For friends who lift me when I'm low,
For family who loves me as I grow.
For laughter shared around the table,
For tears that cleanse and hearts that enable.

Gratitude, the quiet joy we find,
In simple pleasures, in ties that bind.
For every challenge that makes me strong,
For every note of life's sweet song.

So let us pause, with hearts sincere,
To cherish all that we hold dear.
In gratitude, we find our way,
To brighter tomorrows, come what may.

"Satyam Shivam Sundaram"

Beneath the surface, where all truths reside,
"Satyam" reigns, casting an eternal guide.
Unfaltering, steadfast, like the morning sun,
It lights our path until the day is done.

"Shivam" emerges, a serene embrace,
In every soul, a divine trace.
Destroyer of illusion, bestower of grace,
In his silence, we find our place.

"Sundaram" blossoms, beauty untold,
In nature's rhythm and stories old.
A harmony woven through the earth and sky,
A symphony that will never die.

Together they stand, a trinity of light,
"Satyam," "Shivam," shining so bright.
In their unity, we find our way,
Guided by truth, love, and beauty's ray.

In every breath, in every thought,
This sacred mantra we have sought.
"Satyam," "Shivam," "Sundaram," divine and pure,
In their essence, we find our cure.